Dutch Oven & Outdoor Cooking

Kelsey Dollar

The American Pantry Collection ™

Published by:
Apricot Press
Box 98
Nephi, Utah
84648

books@apricotpress.com
www.apricotpress.com

ISBN # 1-885027-40-0

Cover Design & Layout by Erin Allred
Printed in the United States of America

Forward

Cooking with a Dutch Oven is a versatile, exciting way to prepare a meal. Anyone can do it, from the most novice of beginners to a seasoned outdoor chef looking for a challenge. If you are a beginner, this book can be your introduction and guide to some truly wonderful meals. If you are already a Dutch Oven pro, this book will provide more recipes for your arsenal, also feel free to send me your favorites, they might even be feature in my next book! No matter your skill level, the recipes in this book represent hours of research and testing to find the absolute best Dutch Oven recipes around. Additionally, I have included a section on Grilling-since often Dutch Oven cooking and grilling go hand in hand to produce different parts of the outdoor meal. Use this cookbook to produce amazing Dutch Oven and outdoor meals for many years to come. From my Dutch Oven to yours, Enjoy!

Kelsey Dollar

What you will need for Dutch Oven Cooking:

A Dutch Oven- there is a huge variety of choices when selecting a Dutch Oven. I recommend starting with a 12 inch size, which is standard for most recipes. Look for a Dutch Oven with a snug fitting lid and solid construction, you don't want the legs punching through the bottom when its filled with food or the handle breaking off when you're carrying a hot oven full of scalding food! I prefer cast iron to aluminum because they cook food more evenly and retain more heat while cooking. I also prefer the smoky flavor the cast iron gives food!

A Lid Lifter- specific tools are sold commercially, but if you don't want to shell out the big bucks, a large set of pliers will work quite well.

A Heat Source- I say it this way because you have MANY options for heat source. My personal favorite is charcoal briquettes, however, I have seen people use wood chips, logs or even put the whole Dutch Oven in the conventional oven. You can use your Dutch Oven in an above ground fire pit or dig a hole, then place your heat evenly in the hole for great insulation and heat distribution. Basically, anything you can dream up to supply heat to your Dutch Oven will probably work with some experimentation and trial and error. If you want to go the safe, tried and true method, use briquettes for simplicity and predictability.

Long Handed Tongs- makes placing and moving hot coals MUCH easier! If you try to use a stick or metal spoon and such it is very likely you'll get burned and have uneven coal placement, which means burned spots in your food.

Optional tools that make Dutch Oven cooking easier:

Leather Gloves- to protect your hands from the heat

Aluminum Foil- makes clean up a snap. Just line the Dutch Oven and lid with a layer or two of aluminum foil, then add the food and cook as usual. After the meal has been devoured, simply remove the aluminum foil and the mess, no more clean up required!

Small Hand Broom- to sweep off the lid before you open it to keep the ashes and soot from falling into your delicious food.

Meat Thermometer-to more easily cook dishes, particularly meat, to perfection, a meat thermometer is quite useful.

A Charcoal Briquette Chimney- quickly heats the briquettes to use for cooking

How many Dutch Ovens Will You Need?

Determining how many Dutch Ovens it will take to feed your crew can be tricky. First of all, each type of Dutch Oven is made differently with different dimensions and each manufacturer has their own standard sizes. Here is my attempt to compile some wisdom to help you determine how many Dutch Ovens it will take to feed the number of people you're planning on serving.

A 12 inch Dutch Oven is the most common standard size, most recipes are created for this size, and unless noted otherwise, assume all recipes will be prepared in a 12 inch oven. As a general rule, one can plan on a 12 inch Dutch Oven feeding 6 to 8 people, if it's a one dish meal, with protein and starch in the same dish. If you are preparing one 12 inch Dutch Oven with a protein in it, another one with some type of side dish and a third with either a bread or dessert, you could plan on feeding 12 to 15 people, but this of course depends on how many portions of meat, in particular, you prepare in that particular dish.

If you've got a larger group, the easiest thing is to just add more dishes. Instead of just having one choice of protein and one side, maybe you can serve a choice of beef or chicken, then have three sides and so on.

If you're cooking for a smaller group, say 2 or 4 people, you might think a Dutch Oven is too big, but you'd be wrong. Many manufactures make 8, 9, 10 and 11 inch Dutch Ovens and other sized vessels to cook in which can work perfectly for a small group. There are many wonderful one dish meals that combine the protein and side into one Dutch Oven; that way the preparation and clean up are super easy! Those times you're not in the mood for clean up, might I recommend lining the Dutch Oven with aluminum foil, that way clean up is almost nonexistent

Temperature Control

Perhaps the most difficult part of Dutch Oven Cooking is controlling the temperature so the food is cooked properly, not too quickly, but evenly and thoroughly. With practice, you will get a good feel for how much heat is required to cook various dishes in a variety of weather conditions. Dutch Oven cooking can be done in any climate, even snow and wind, if the proper adjustments are made. If you are unfamiliar or out of practice cooking with a Dutch Oven, here are some general guidelines.

First of all, use good quality briquettes or wood, because the food is contained inside a vessel, scents and flavors are unnecessary in your wood chips or briquettes and will never reach the food. When using briquettes, the temperature is more easily controlled than when using wood because the briquettes burn more consistently and evenly, but wood chips are fun and challenging in their own way. Because I primarily use briquettes, that is the medium of cooking I am most familiar with, so I have the most useful information about briquettes. Each briquette will emit roughly 10 to 15 degrees of heat. As your conditions change, the temperature will also change, for example, if you're cooking on a windy day, the wind brings more oxygen to the coals, so they burn faster and hotter. But, in general, you can plan on about 10-15 degrees of heat per coal. It is not an exact science, but a good rule of thumb to use as a base for Dutch Oven cooking.

For most Dutch Oven cooking, it is important to space coals properly on the top and bottom of the Dutch Oven; focus the heat around the edges, near the rim or lip of the top and bottom of the Dutch Oven, I usually make a ring around the top and bottom of the vessel (coals in the middle of the Dutch oven create hot spots and can leave some parts burned and others raw in the same dish). Arrange the bulk of the heat on the bottom, because heat naturally rises; a good guide is for every two coals you put beneath the Dutch Oven, put one on the lid- adjust these numbers as you see fit, but it is a good place to start. The exceptions to this are boiling and slow roasting. For boiling and simmering, it is usually best to put all the heat below the cooking vessel. For slow roasting, the heat should be evenly spaced above and below the Dutch Oven.

Keep in mind that as the coals burn, they gradually become smaller and therefore give off less heat; it is a good idea to have a chimney starter or fire pit going in addition to the coals you are using for cooking, that way, when your coals start to cool, you can replace them with newer, hotter ones. It takes about 30 minutes from the time they are lit for most coals to reach optimal temperature.

An important thing to remember is, you can always add more heat if your food is not cooking quickly enough, but if too much heat is added, food will be burned and that is hard to fix. If you're unsure of cooking temperature, start with less heat and work up to keep from burning and ruining your meal. It may take a bit longer, but at least you'll get a well cooked meal in the end, rather than ending up with inedible carbon where your food should have been!

Meat Temperature Guidelines

When cooking or grilling meat, many people are unsure of proper internal temperature for both safety and doneness preference. For accurate temperature readings, be sure that the thermometer is in a thick section of the meat and not touching any bone. Measure temperature immediately following removal from heat source; if left to properly rest, meat temperatures can rise as much as 30 degrees. Here is a guide to ensure optimal taste and texture.

Beef and Lamb: Ground meats should always be heated to at least 160 degrees to ensure safety.
Rare: 125-130 degrees
Medium-Rare:130-140 degrees
Medium: 140-155 degrees
Medium Well: 155 to 165 degrees
Well Done: 165 and above

Pork: It is not recommended that pork be cooked to less than 140 degrees.
Medium: 140-155 degrees
Medium Well: 155-165 degrees
Well Done: 175-185 degrees

Poultry: Poultry such as chicken and turkey should always be cooked to at least 160 degrees.
Dark meat: 170-175
White Meat: 160-165

Fish: Fish should always be cooked to an internal temperature of at least 120 degrees.
Medium Rare: 120 degrees
Rare: 125-135 degrees
Medium: 135-140 degrees

Breakfast From the Dutch Oven

Cheese Breakfast Biscuits

2 Cups Biscuit Mix
1 lb Breakfast Sausage, crumbled
2/3 Cup Milk
2 Cups Cheese, shredded

Generously oil a 12 inch Dutch Oven and heat. Combine all ingredients and mix well. Drop by large spoonfuls into heated Dutch Oven. Cover and cook for 25 minutes, until biscuit edges are browned. Remove from Dutch Oven and drain excess oil.

Breakfast Casserole

3 Tbsp Butter
8 Baked Potatoes, grated
1 lb Bacon, sliced or cubed
1 lb Button Mushrooms, sliced
1 Onion, diced
10 Eggs
8 oz Cream Cheese
1 lb Cheddar Cheese, shredded

Melt butter in a 12 inch Dutch Oven over medium heat. Add potatoes and cook until browned, then remove and set them aside. Wipe out Dutch Oven with a paper towel, then add bacon and fry until crispy. Drain bacon and crumble. Drain excess grease and add onions and mushrooms to bacon grease. Sauté until onions are clear and mushrooms are limp. In a separate bowl, scramble eggs, then pour over onion and mushrooms, cook until eggs are just starting to solidify but still wet. Remove eggs from Dutch Oven then spread potatoes in the bottom of Dutch Oven and spread eggs on top. Sprinkle eggs with bacon and spread cream cheese over bacon. Top with cheese then bake over medium hot coals for 20 minutes, or until cheese is melted and bubbly around the edges.

Catch of the Day Breakfast Casserole

3+ Fish Fillets, boned and skinned
1/2 tsp Lemon Pepper
Salt and Pepper
10 Eggs, beaten
1 Onion, diced
3Tbsp Vegetable Oil
5 Cups Hashed Browns
1 Cup Salsa

Heat a 12 inch Dutch Oven over medium heat. Sprinkle fish fillets with lemon pepper, salt and black pepper then set aside. Pour eggs and onions into Dutch Oven and cook, stirring frequently, until eggs are solid and onions are clear. Remove eggs and set aside. Add oil to Dutch Oven and layer 1/3 of potatoes, then 1/3 eggs and 1/3 of fish fillets then repeat twice more. Cover Dutch Oven and cook for 30 minutes, until fish is cooked through. Serve topped with salsa.

Mountain Man Breakfast

1 1/2 lbs Sausage
1 Onion, chopped
10 Potatoes, baked and grated
12 Eggs
1 1/2 lbs Cheese, shredded
12 oz Salsa
12 Flour Tortillas

Heat a 12 inch Dutch Oven over medium high heat. Crumble sausage into Dutch Oven and add onions, cook until browned. Remove sausage and onions and set aside. Drain grease, leaving 2 tablespoons. Add potatoes and fry until browned. Add Sausage and onions to potatoes then toss to combine. In a separate bowl, beat eggs then pour over potato mixture in Dutch Oven. Cover and bake for 20 minutes, stirring occasionally, until eggs become mostly solidified, but still wet. Sprinkle with cheese and cook for an additional 15 minutes. Serve with salsa and tortillas.

The Lot Breakfast

1/2 lb Sausage
1/2 lb Ham
8 oz Mushrooms, quartered
1 Yellow Onion, diced
1 Bell Pepper, diced
4 Medium Potatoes, diced
12 Eggs, beaten
1/2 Cup Milk
1 tsp Salt
1/2 tsp Ground Black Pepper
2 Cups Grated Cheddar Cheese

In a 12 inch Dutch Oven over medium heat, brown sausage. Add ham, mushrooms, onion, bell pepper and potatoes; cover and cook for 10 to 15 minutes stirring occasionally. In a mixing bowl, combine eggs, milk salt and pepper and beat until well combined. Pour egg mixture over meat and veggies then add half the cheese; stir to combine. Cook for 5 minutes then stir so the bottom doesn't burn. Top with remaining cheese and continue cooking until eggs are set and cheese is melted.

The World's Best Dutch Oven Beef and Pork Recipes

BBQ Meatloaf

Sauce:
1-8 oz can Tomato Sauce
2 Tbsp BBQ Sauce
1 tsp Mustard
2 Tbsp Brown Sugar

Meatloaf:
1 1/2 lbs Ground Beef
1 Egg
1/2 Cup Oatmeal
2 Tbsp BBQ Sauce
2 Tbsp Ketchup
1 tsp Mustard
1 Garlic Clove, minced
2 Tbsp Dry Onion
2 tsp Brown Sugar

Brush a 12 inch Dutch Oven with oil then set aside. In a medium saucepan, combine sauce ingredients and simmer for 5 minutes then set aside. In a mixing bowl, combine egg, oatmeal, BBQ sauce, ketchup, mustard, garlic, onions and brown sugar then let rest for 15 minutes. Add hamburger and knead until well combined and it will hold its shape. Roll into a log and place, in the shape of a ring, inside the Dutch Oven. Cover and cook over medium high heat for 20 minutes. Drain excess grease, then drizzle sauce over the meatloaf ring. Remove coals from under Dutch Oven and cook with only coals on the lid for 35 minutes, until ground beef is browned.

Kickin' Corned Beef

4 lbs Corned Beef Brisket
1/2 Cup Onion, chopped
2 Cloves Garlic, minced
2 Bay Leaves
6 Potatoes, pared
5 Carrots, pared
1 Head Cabbage, chopped into wedges
Prepared Mustard
1/4 Cup Brown Sugar
Dash Ground Cloves

Place corned beef in 12 inch Dutch Oven then add hot water, just enough to cover brisket. Add onion, garlic and bay leaves. Cover and simmer for 4 hours, until meat is tender. Remove meat from Dutch Oven. Place potatoes and carrots in Dutch Oven; cover, then bring to a boil. Simmer for 10 minutes. Add cabbage and cook an additional 20 minutes. While vegetables are cooking, spread a thin layer of mustard on the fat side of brisket, sprinkle with brown sugar and cloves. Put meat in a separate Dutch Oven and cook for an additional 30 minutes, checking frequently for signs of drying out.

Liver and Onions

1/4 Cup Bacon Grease
2 lbs Baby Beef Liver
Salt and Pepper
1 Cup Flour
2 Large Onions

Over medium high heat, warm bacon grease in a 12 inch Dutch Oven. Clean and trim liver then slice into 4 pieces. Season pieces with salt and pepper then dredge in flour. Brown liver in bacon grease on all sides, then reduce heat to medium; cover and simmer. Slice onions then add to liver. Simmer for 45 minutes turning ever 15 minutes to prevent sticking.

BBQ Steak Sandwich

2 Tbsp Butter
1 1/2 lbs Round Steak, sliced into thin strips
1/4 Cup Chili Sauce
1/4 Cup Lemon Juice
1/4 Cup Beef Stock
2 Tbsp Brown Sugar
1/2 tsp Salt
1/4 tsp Paprika
1 Tbsp Worcestershire Sauce
1 Clove Garlic, minced
1 tsp Horseradish
2 Tbsp Dried Onion
1/4 tsp Red Pepper
1 1/2 Tbsp Cornstarch
6 Slices Cheddar Cheese
6 Sandwich Buns

In a 12 inch Dutch Oven over medium heat, melt butter then brown steak. Reduce heat to low and add chili sauce, lemon juice, 1/8 cup beef stock, brown sugar, salt, paprika, Worcestershire sauce, garlic, horseradish, onion and red pepper. Cover and simmer for 60 minutes, stirring occasionally. In a separate bowl, combine remaining 1/4 cup beef stock and corn starch and mix until smooth. Add corn starch to beef and cook, stirring frequently, until sauce thickens. Butter the insides of the buns and brown on a hot grill then top with steak and cheddar cheese.

Mushroom Swiss Steak

1/4 Cup Canola Oil
3 lbs Round Steak
Salt and Pepper
Flour
1-8 oz can Mushrooms
1-10.5 oz can Cream of Mushroom Soup
1/2 Cup Milk

In a 12 inch Dutch Oven, heat canola oil over medium heat. Clean and trim fat from steaks then sprinkle with salt and pepper then coat with flour. Pound the flour into the steaks and tenderize the meat. Add steaks to oil and brown one each side. Reduce the heat and simmer for 35 minutes. In a separate saucepan, combine mushrooms, soup and milk and mix until smooth. Pour soup mixture over steaks, cover and continue cooking for 90 minutes, until steaks are tender.

Ranch Pork Chops

1/4 Cup Oil
8 Pork Chops
1/4 Cup Flour
1 Cup Water
2 Tbsp Brown Sugar
1/4 Cup Onion, chopped
1 tsp Garlic Powder
3 Tbsp Ketchup
1/2 Cup Sour Cream

In a 12 inch Dutch Oven, heat oil. Dredge pork chops in flour then brown in hot oil. Add water, brown sugar, onions, garlic powder and ketchup. Cover and simmer for 30 minutes. Remove from heat and mix in sour cream.

Poultry and Fish

Roasted Orange Chicken

5 lbs Roasting Chicken
3 Tbsp Canola Oil, divided
2 Tbsp Soy Sauce
1 Tbsp Salt
1 tsp White Pepper
1 Tbsp Sugar
1 Tbsp Garlic Powder
1 Tbsp Crushed Basil
1 tsp Ground Ginger
2 Onions, quartered
1 Orange, cut into Wedges

Preheat oven to 500 degrees. Clean and rinse chicken, trim excess fat. In a bowl, combine 2 Tbsp oil and soy sauce, whisk until well combined. In a bag, combine salt, pepper, sugar, garlic powder, basil and ginger and mix well. Use your hand to loosen chicken skin, leaving skin in tact as much as possible; carefully spread a thin layer of oil mixture between skin and meat and inside the chicken. Rub spice mix under skin. Stuff chest cavity with half of the quartered onionsand oranges. Spread the remaining tablespoon of canola oil over outside skin of chicken. Place chickens, breast down in a 12 inch Dutch Oven. Surround with remaining orange and onion. Cover and bake for 50 to 60 minutes. Uncover and bake an additional 15 to 20 minutes. Let chicken rest for 10 to 15 minutes then serve.

Cowboy Creole Chicken

8 Chicken Breasts
1 tsp Garlic Powder
1/2 lb Sliced Bacon, chopped
1 lb Ham, diced
1 Onion, Chopped
1 Tbsp Parsley
1/2 tsp Thyme
2 Cups Boiling Water
2 Cups Stewed Tomatoes
1 tsp Salt
1/4 tsp Tabasco Sauce
1/2 Cup Celery, chopped
3 Tbsp Corn Starch
1/4 Cup Cold Water

Heat a 14 inch Dutch Oven. Wash chicken and pat dry. Sprinkle garlic powder over chicken and set aside. Place bacon in Dutch Oven and cook until crispy. Remove bacon and set aside. Brown chicken in bacon grease, then remove and set aside. Add ham and onions to Dutch Oven and cook until ham is brown and onions are limp. Add chicken and bacon back to Dutch Oven then add parsley, thyme, water, stewed tomatoes, salt, Tabasco and celery. Cover and cook for 45 minutes on a low simmer. In a small bowl, combine corn starch and cold water until smooth. Remove meat and veggies from liquid and pour in cornstarch mixture. Cook, stirring frequently, until liquid thickens into gravy. Serve chicken and veggies smothered in gravy.

Cowboy Fish

2 lbs Fish*, boned and skinned
1/2 Cup Vegetable Oil
3 Tbsp Lemon Pepper
1/2 to 1 Cup Flour

Heat a large cast iron skillet over medium high to high heat. Combine oil and lemon pepper then pour into frying pan. Heat oil for a few minutes to blacken the lemon pepper, then reduce the heat to medium. Dredge fish in flour and fry for 8 to 10 minutes, turning once.

*My favorite fish to use for this dish is freshly caught catfish, but feel free to use your favorite.

Pineapple Apricot Chicken

3 lbs Boneless, Skinless Chicken Breast
1 Cup Pineapple Apricot Preserve
1 Cup French Catalina Salad Dressing
1 1 oz packed Dry Onion Soup Mix

Place chicken breast pieces in a 12 inch Dutch Oven and set aside. In a mixing bowl, combine preserves, dressing and soup mix then stir until combined. Pour sauce over chicken and mix to coat. Cover and cook at 350 degrees for 1 hour, until chicken is cooked through.

Teriyaki Chicken

4 Roasting Chickens
1/4 Cup Peanut Oil
1 Onion, sliced
2 1/2 Cups Brown Sugar
12 oz Teriyaki Sauce

Rinse chicken then cut into breast, thigh, leg and wing pieces. Pour oil into a 12 inch Dutch Oven then arrange chicken in the bottom. Spread sliced onions over chicken. Sprinkle the chicken with brown sugar, then pour teriyaki sauce on top. Cover Dutch Oven and cook for 60 minutes.

Happy Chicken

6 Boneless, Skinless Chicken Breasts
1 Onion, sliced
1 Bell Pepper, seeded and sliced
8 oz Brown Sugar Bacon*
1 Cup Buttermilk
1 Can Cream of Chicken Soup
1 Can Cream of Mushroom Soup
4 Large Potatoes, peeled and sliced
4 Medium Carrots, peeled and sliced
1/4 tsp Garlic Salt
2 Tbsp Canola Oil

In a 16 inch Dutch Oven, heat oil to 350-400 degrees. Add onion, bell pepper, bacon and mushroom; sauté for 5 minutes. Add potatoes and carrots and cook for an additional 4 minutes. Add remaining ingredients then lower the heat to 300 degrees. Cook for 90 minutes, stirring every 15 to 20 minutes, until potatoes are cooked through.

*If you can't find brown sugar bacon, maple will work as well, brown sugar is more of a subtle flavor. If you use maple bacon, only use 6 ounces so it does not over power the other flavors of the dish.

Soups, Stews and Casseroles for the Dutch Oven

Camper's Casserole

1 lb Ground Beef
1 Cup Celery, chopped
4 Cups Zucchini, chopped
Salt and Pepper
8 oz Tomato Sauce
1 Tbsp Sugar
3 Tbsp Worcestershire Sauce
1/4 Cup Parmesan Cheese, grated

Heat 12 inch Dutch Oven, add meat and cook until brown. Add celery and cook until celery is wilted. Remove meat mixture and set aside. Place zucchini in Dutch Oven and sauté until lightly browned. Add meat mixture back into zucchini. Salt and pepper to taste. In a separate bowl, combine Worcestershire sauce, sugar and tomato sauce then pour over meat mixture. Spread top with cheese. Cook over low fire for 30 minutes, until casserole is bubbly.

Chili Blanco

1 1/2 lbs Chicken Breast, cubed
1 Yellow Onion, diced
1 Cup Chicken Stock
1-4 oz can Diced Green Chiles
2 tsp Cumin
3-15 oz cans White Beans (I prefer Great Northern)
1/4 tsp Red Pepper
Salt and Pepper
1 Cup Sour Cream
1 Cup Monterey Jack Cheese

Brush the bottom of a 12 inch Dutch Oven with oil, then heat over medium heat. Add chicken and onion and cook until chicken is browned and onions are translucent. Add chicken stock, green chilies, cumin, beans, red pepper and salt and pepper. Mix to combine and bring to a simmer. Cover and simmer for 35 minutes, stirring occasionally. Mix in sour cream and cheese and heat through. Serve with bread or tortilla chips.

Pot of Yummy

1 1/2 lbs Ground Beef
3-8 oz cans Tomato Sauce
1-15 oz can Corn, drained
1 White Onion, diced
16 oz Dry Pasta (shells or elbow macaroni are my favorites)
3 Cups Water
1 tsp Dried Basil
1 tsp Ground Oregano
1 tsp Chili Powder
1 1/2 tsp Sugar
Salt and Pepper
1 1/2 Cups Shredded Cheddar Cheese

Heat a 12 inch Dutch Oven over medium heat. Brown ground beef then drain fat. Add onion and cook until it becomes translucent. Add tomato sauce, corn, onion, pasta, water and spices. Simmer, uncovered, for 30 minutes, stirring occasionally. Top with cheese and serve.

Mediterranean Casserole

1 lb Noodles or Spaghetti
2 Tbsp Cooking Oil
2 lbs Ground Beef
1 Medium Onion, chopped
1 can Tomato Sauce
1/2 can Water
1 can Peas- drained
1 tsp Salt
1/2 tsp Pepper
1/2 tsp Oregano
1/2 lb shredded or cubed mozzarella

In a large pot of boiling water, cook noodles according to package directions. Drain and set aside. In 14 inch Dutch Oven, heat oil then brown ground beef and onion. Add tomato sauce, water, peas, salt, pepper, oregano, half of cheese and noodles and mix until combined. Top with remaining cheese, cover and cook over medium coals until cheese is melted and bubbly.

Split Pea Soup

2 1/2 Cups Water
2 Cups Dry Split Peas
1 Yellow Onion, chopped
1/2 lb Bacon
1 tsp Salt

Rinse the peas, pick through them and remove un-wanted pieces. Soak the peas in water for at least 6 hours, or overnight. Cut bacon into bite sized pieces. In a 12 inch Dutch Oven, combine peas with remaining water, onions, bacon and salt. Cook over 300 degree heat for 3 hours.

Pepper Pot Beef Stew

3 lbs Lean Stewing Meat
Salt
3 Cups Beef Stock
1 Cup Green Beans
3 Stalks Celery
3 Large Carrots
4 Medium Potatoes
1 Large Red Onion
1/2 tsp Ground Black Pepper

Heat Dutch Oven over 350 degree heat. Trim excess fat from meat and cube into 1/2 to 1 inch pieces. Place meat in Dutch Oven and sprinkle with salt. Cook for 5 to 7 minutes, until meat is becoming brown. Add beef stock, cover and cook for 50 minutes. Chop vegetables into bite sized pieces then add to Dutch Oven. Sprinkle with ground pepper and cook for 60 minutes- until vegetables are soft and tender.

Turkey Chowder

2 Turkey Legs
6 Medium Potatoes, cubed
2 Medium Carrots, chopped
2 Stalks Celery, chopped with their tops
1 Medium Onion, diced
16 oz Frozen Corn
1/8 Cup Fresh Basil Leaves
2 tsp Salt
1/4 tsp Pepper
1/2 Cup Grated Parmesan Cheese
2 Cups Milk
1/4 Cup Flour

Fill a 12 inch Dutch Oven 3⁄4 full with water and bring
to a boil. Add turkey, potatoes, carrots, celery, onion,
corn, basil, salt and pepper and simmer for 90 minutes.
In a mixing bowl, combine parmesan, milk and flour
and mix until smooth. Add milk mixture to Dutch Oven
and continue to simmer until cheese softens and liquid
thickens.

Kielbasa Casserole

1 lb Kielbasa
4 Medium Potatoes
2 Apples, peeled
2 Cans Sauerkraut, washed and drained
1 Cup Apple Juice

Heat a 12 inch Dutch Oven over medium high heat.
Slice Kielbasa into 1/2 inch slices, then brown in Dutch
Oven. Cube potatoes and apples then add to Kielbasa
along with sauerkraut and apple juice. Stir to combine,
then cover and simmer for 45 minutes, until apples and
potatoes are tender.

Dutch Oven Bread

Fry Bread (Scones)

1 Cup Warm Water
1 Tbsp Yeast
1 Tbsp Sugar
3 Cups Flour
1/4 Cup Vegetable Oil
1 tsp Salt
Vegetable Oil for frying

In a large mixing bowl, combine warm water, yeast and sugar and stir to dissolve sugar; set aside for 5 minutes. Add flour, one cup at a time, mixing between each cup. Mix in 1/4 cup vegetable oil and mix until oil is incorporated and a nice dough ball is formed. Cover and let dough rise for 30 minutes. Heat cooking oil to around 375 degrees. Roll dough into golf ball sized rounds, then flatten balls into discs and drop into hot oil. Fry until dough browns on one side, then flip and brown the other side. Drain bread on paper towels, then serve with honey butter as scones, or with chili and toppings as Navajo Tacos. This dough can also be used to make a quick and easy pizza dough, top with marinara sauce, cheese and your favorite toppings!

Yeast Rolls

2 1/4 tsp Dry Yeast
1 Tbsp Sugar
1/2 tsp Salt
1 Egg
3 Tbsp Oil
1 Cup Milk, warmed
2 1/2 to 3 Cups Flour

Lightly oil 12 inch Dutch Oven and set aside. In a large mixing bowl, dissolve sugar in warm milk. Add yeast and gently stir until dissolved. Add egg, salt and oil then mix until well combined. Add 1 1/2 Cups of flour and beat vigorously until dough is smooth. Add remaining flour 1/2 cup at a time while kneading and mixing with hands, until dough becomes soft and stops sticking to sides of bowl. Cover and let raise until dough has doubled in size.

Divide dough into tablespoon size balls. Place dough balls in Dutch Oven, cover and let raise again until size has doubled. Bake for 25 to 30 minutes, rotating pot one quarter turn every 10 minutes. Rolls are done when the tops are lightly browned and dough pulls away from sides of pot.

Old Fashioned Baking Powder Biscuits

1/2 Cup Shortening
1 Tbsp Sugar
1 tsp Salt
2 Cups Flour
3 tsp Baking Powder
3/4 Cups Milk

Oil a 14 inch Dutch Oven and set aside. Place shortening in a large mixing bowl then cut in sugar, salt, flour and baking powder. Add milk and mix until combined. Knead dough for about 2 minutes. Flour a cutting board or other clean surface and dump dough onto flour. Roll dough until 1/4 inch thickness. Cut biscuits into circles then place in Dutch Oven an inch apart and cook over very hot coals for about 12 minutes.

Cinnamon Raisin Bread

2 Cups Milk
4 1/2 Cups + 2 Tbsp Sugar plus
1 tsp Salt
1/4 Cup Shortening
1/4 Cup Warm Water
5 tsp Dry, Active Yeast
6 Cups Flour
1/4 Cup Butter, softened
2 tsp Cinnamon
1/3 Cup Raisins

In a medium pan, heat milk until bubbles appear at edges, do not boil. In a separate bowl, cut 4 1/2 cups sugar and salt into shortening. Add milk and mix until well combined. Warm water then add yeast and stir to dissolve. Pour yeast water into milk mixture and beat until incorporated. Add flour 1/2 cup at a time, mixing until a stiff dough is formed. Flour a clean surface and knead for 7 to 10 minutes, until dough becomes smooth. Loosely cover and let raise for 1 hour. Punch down dough then divide in half. Roll dough into two balls then roll out to 1/2 inch thickness. Spread dough with butter, sprinkle with cinnamon, then sugar and top with raisins. Roll and place in a 16 inch Dutch Oven seam side down. Let bread raise until size is doubled. Bake over medium hot coals for 45 to 60 minutes, until bread is golden brown.

Sopapillas

1 Envelope Dry Yeast (2 1/4 tsp)
1/2 Cup Warm Water
3 Cups Flour
1/2 tsp Salt
1 Tbsp Canola Oil
1 Egg
Honey
Sugar
Cinnamon

In a small mixing bowl, dissolve yeast in the warm water, set aside. In a large mixing bowl, combine flour and salt. Add egg and oil and stir until ingredients are incorporated. On a lightly floured surface, knead for 5 minutes. Place back in mixing bowl, cover and let raise for two hours until dough has doubled in size. Turn dough onto lightly floured surface and roll to 1/2 inch thickness. Cut into 1 1/2 inch squares and let raise for another 90 minutes. In a 16 inch Dutch Oven, heat 2 quarts of oil. Add dough squares and cook both sides until golden brown. Drain grease then toss with cinnamon and sugar. Serve hot with honey.

Marley's Biscuits

2 Cups Flour
1 Cup Whole Wheat Flour
5 tsp Baking Powder
1 tsp Salt
1/2 Cup Shortening
1 Cup Buttermilk

In a large bowl, combine dry ingredients. Add shortening, cut with a pastry knife or a fork until it becomes a coarse meal. Add buttermilk and mix 12 strokes (dough should still be slightly lumpy, but most of the lumps should be incorporated). Scoop out spoonfuls of dough, roll into 1/2 inch balls. Place balls in a16 inch Dutch Oven and bake over 350 degree heat for 12 to 15 minutes, until biscuits are cooked through.

Cheesy Bread

2 1/2 to 3 Cups All Purpose Flour
1 tsp salt
1 1/2 Tbsp Sugar
1 pkg Active Dry Yeast
3/4 Cup Milk
1/4 Cup Water
2 Tbsp Butter, softened
1/4 Cup Butter, melted
1/2 tsp Paprika
1/4 tsp Celery Seed
1 Tbsp Dried Onion
1/2 tsp Oregano
1/4 tsp Garlic Salt
1/4 Cup Butter, melted
1 Cup Shredded Cheddar Cheese

In a large mixing bowl, combine 2 1/2 cups flour, salt, sugar and yeast. Mix to combine and set aside. In a 12 inch Dutch Oven, combine milk and water with two tablespoons butter and heat until butter is melted. Add flour mixture and mix well. Turn dough onto well floured surface and knead for 5 minutes. Cover and let rise until doubled in size. Grease Dutch Oven and spread dough into bottom. In a separate bowl, combine paprika, celery seed, dried onion, oregano, garlic salt and 1/4 cup melted butter then spread over dough. Sprinkle cheese over the top, cover and allow to rise until doubled in size again. Bake over hot coals at 375 degrees for 25 minutes.

Vegetables and Side Dishes

Brian's Baked Beans

1 lb Bacon
1 Onion, chopped
5 Cans Pork and Beans
2 1/2 Cups Brown Sugar

Heat 12 inch Dutch Oven over hot coals or on a cook stove. Cut bacon into bite sized pieces and place in hot Dutch Oven. Add onion and sauté until onions are clear and limp and fat is cooked on bacon. Add pork and beans and brown sugar, mix until combined. Cover Dutch oven and cook until heated through.

Ranch House Potatoes

4 lbs Red Potatoes
1 Cup Butter
1 pkg Dry Ranch Dressing Seasoning Mix

Cube or quarter potatoes into a 12 inch Dutch Oven. Spread butter over the top of the potatoes then sprinkle with seasoning packet. Bake over 350 degree coals for about 60 minutes, until potatoes are soft and edges are slightly golden.

Dutch Oven Potato Casserole

1/2 Cup Butter
1/2 Yellow Onion, diced
1- 10.5 oz can Cream of Chicken Soup
1-10.5 oz can Cream of Mushroom Soup
1 Cup Sour Cream
Salt and Pepper
2 Cups Shredded Cheese
1 1/2 to 2 lbs Frozen Hashed Browns

Crumble:
2 Cups Crushed Corn Flakes
2 Tbsp Parsley Flakes
1/4 Cup Butter, melted

Melt butter in a 12 inch Dutch Oven over medium heat. Add onions and cook until tender. Add soup, sour cream, half of cheese, salt and pepper then mix until smooth. Fold in hashed browns then top with remaining cheese. In a separate bowl, combine ingredients for crumble and sprinkle over potatoes. Cover and cook over medium low heat for about 30 minutes, until cheese is melted and hashed browns are cooked through.

Saucy Potatoes with Bacon

1 lb Bacon
1 large Onion, chopped
6 Garlic Cloves, minced
1 pint fresh mushrooms, quartered
5 lbs Potatoes, cubed
1-10 1/2 oz can Cream of Chicken Soup
1-10 1/2 oz can Condensed Cheddar Cheese Soup
1 Cup Sour Cream
2 Tbsp Worcestershire Sauce
1 Tbsp Soy Sauce
Salt and Pepper

Cut bacon to bite sized pieces. In a 12 inch Dutch Oven over medium-hot coals, brown bacon then add onions, garlic and mushrooms. Cook, stirring frequently, until onions and mushrooms are tender, then add potatoes. In a mixing bowl, combine remaining ingredients and mix until well combined; dump sauce mixture over potatoes in Dutch oven and stir until veggies are well coated. Cook at about 350 degrees for 75 minutes, stirring every 15 minutes to keep cooking even.

Old Fashioned Sweet Yams

3 lbs Yams or Sweet Potatoes, peeled
2 Cups Sugar
1 1/2 Cups Margarine
1 Cup Marshmallow Cream
15 oz Crushed Pineapple
1 tsp Dry Orange Peel
1 tsp Allspice
1/2 tsp Nutmeg
1/4 tsp Cinnamon

Slice yams into 1/4 inch thick rounds. Place in a greased Dutch Oven and cook covered over 400 degree heat for 10-15 minutes, until yams begin to get tender. Remove yams from Dutch Oven and lower heat to 250 degrees. In the Dutch Oven, layer yams, then sugar, butter and pineapple; each layer should be sprinkled with spices. Repeat layering twice more, so you end up with 3 layers. Cover and cook for 30 minutes until yams are soft and gooey.

Italian Garden Dutch Oven

1/4 Cup Butter
6 Small Zucchini
1 Medium Cauliflower
1 Green Pepper
1 Medium Onion
1 Cup Mushroom halves
1 tsp Dry Minced Garlic
Salt and Pepper
3 Roma Tomatoes
1/2 Cup Parmesan Cheese

Chop all vegetables into bite sized pieces. Melt butter in the Dutch Oven. Add zucchini, cauliflower, green pepper, onion, mushrooms, garlic, salt and pepper then sauté for 4 minutes. Add tomatoes then cover and cook for 15 minutes, until vegetables are desired tenderness. Top with parmesan cheese.

Desserts: The perfect finish for a Dutch Oven Meal

Easy Peach Cobbler

1 large Can Sliced Peaches, with juice
1 pkg dry Yellow Cake Mix
1/2 Cup Butter, frozen
1-2 tsp Cinnamon

Grease a 12 inch Dutch Oven. Pour peaches into Dutch Oven and cover with dry cake mix. Use a grater to grate the butter over the top of the cake mix and spread evenly. Sprinkle cinnamon over the top. Cover and bake over 350 degree coals for 40 minutes.
* For a cakier cobbler, just prepare the cake mix as directed, then spread over peaches, top with 1/4 cup grated butter and cinnamon. Either way, you can't go wrong!

Chocolate Chip Pumpkin Cake

1 1/4 Cup Sugar
1/2 Cup Vegetable Oil
3 Eggs
1 Cup Pumpkin Puree
3/4 Cup Milk
2 1/2 Cups Flour
3 Tbsp Baking Powder
1 tsp Baking Soda
1 1/2 Tbsp Cinnamon
1 1/2 tsp Pumpkin Pie Spice
1/2 tsp Salt
1 Cup Semi Sweet Chocolate Chips

Grease and flour the bottom and sides of a 12 inch Dutch Oven and set aside. In a mixing bowl, combine sugar and oil and mix until sugar is dissolved. Add eggs, pumpkinm puree and milk and mix until well blended. In a separate bowl, mix flour, baking powder, baking soda, cinnamon, pumpkin pie spice and salt and mix to combine then add to wet ingredients. Beat for 4 minutes, until well blended then fold in chocolate chips. Pour batter into prepared Dutch Oven and cook over 350 degree coals for 35 to 40 minutes. Cakes cook best with more coals on the lid than underneath, it prevents scorching on the bottom. Remove Dutch Oven from heat, remove lid and allow to cool for 15 minutes. Use a knife or spatula to loosen cake from sides of Dutch Oven and invert onto a plate. Serve warm or let cool and frost with chocolate frosting.

Upside Down Pineapple Cake

1/2 Cup Butter
1 1/2 Cups Dark Brown Sugar
1-20 oz can Pineapple Rings
10 Maraschino Cherries
1 pkg Pineapple Cake Mix (Yellow cake mix can be substituted in a pinch.)*
1 1/3 Cups Pineapple Juice
1/3 Cup Oil
3 Eggs

Heat a 12 inch Dutch Oven. Melt butter in the bottom of the Dutch Oven then remove from heat. Sprinkle brown sugar over butter as evenly as you can. Arrange pineapple rings in a single layer along the bottom and sides of Dutch Oven with a cherry in the center of each ring. In a separate bowl, combine cake mix, juice, oil and eggs and mix until combined, do not over mix, it should still be slightly lumpy.

Pour cake batter over pineapple in Dutch Oven and cook over medium hot coals for 30 to 40 minutes, until toothpick inserted into center comes out clean. Remove from coals and let cool for 15 minutes. Serve upside down on a serving plate.

Molten Fudge Cake

1/2 Cup Cocoa Powder
1 Cup Brown Sugar
2 Cups Water
1 pkg Mini Marshmallows
1 Chocolate Fudge Cake Mix
1 Cup Pecans, chopped
1 pkg Chocolate Chips
Whipped Cream

In a 12 inch Dutch Oven, combine cocoa powder, brown sugar and water, mix until well incorporated. Pour marshmallows evenly over the top. Prepare cake mix according to package directions and spread over marshmallows. Top with pecans and chocolate chips. Cover and cook over medium 350 degrees. Serve with whipped cream.

Sour Cream Cake

3/4 Cup Butter, softened
2 Cups Sugar
2 Eggs
1 tsp Vanilla
2 Cups Flour
1 tsp Baking Powder
1/2 tsp Salt
1 Cup Sour Cream
2/3 Cup Brown Sugar
1 tsp Cinnamon
1/2 Cup Pecans, chopped

Grease a 10 inch Dutch Oven and set aside. In a separate bowl, cream butter and sugar together. Add eggs and vanilla then beat until well blended. Stir in flour, baking powder and salt, then mix until completely incorporated. Add sour cream and mix until well blended. Pour half of batter into Dutch Oven then top with brown sugar, cinnamon and pecans then cover with remaining batter. Cover and cook over medium coals for 75 minutes, until bread pulls away from sided of Dutch Oven.

Glaze:
1/2 Cup Evaporated Milk
1 tsp Vanilla
1/4 Cup Powdered Sugar
Combine all ingredients and spread over the top of Sour Cream Cake.

Pumpkin Pie Dessert

Filling:
1-29 oz Can Pumpkin
1 Tbsp Pumpkin Pie Spice
3 Eggs
1 Cup Sugar
1/2 tsp Salt
1 tsp Vanilla
1 Cup Evaporated Milk
Crumble Topping:
1 Dry Yellow Cake Mix
1 Cup Butter, softened
1 Cup Chopped Pecans-optional

Lightly grease a 12 inch Dutch Oven. To make filling, combine pumpkin, pumpkin pie spice, eggs, sugar, salt, vanilla and milk, then mix to combine. Pour into greased Dutch Oven and set aside. To make crumble topping, cut softened butter into cake mix until combined. Then stir in nuts if you are using them. Sprinkle crumble over filling. Cover and cook at 350 for 1 hour, until filling is set. Serve with whipped cream or ice cream.

Grilling: The Perfect Compliment for a Dutch Oven Meal

Teriyaki Steak

3 lbs Sirloin Beef
1/2 Cup Soy Sauce
2 Tbsp Brown Sugar
1 Clove of Garlic
1 Small Piece Gingerroot

Freeze beef; slice thinly across grain. In a large glass bowl, combine soy sauce, brown sugar, garlic and ginger root. Marinate beef in soy sauce mixture for 60 minutes. Heat coals and grill to hot. Remove meat from marinade then grill 4 inches from hot coals for 7 – 9 minutes on each side. Serve immediately.

Patio Steak Barbecue

8 oz Tomato Sauce
1/2 Cup Steak Sauce or A-1
1/4 Cup Prepared Horseradish
2 Tbsp Cider Vinegar
2 Tbsp Brown Sugar
4 Club Steaks, about 1 inch thick
1 tsp Monosodium Glutamate

In a saucepan, combine tomato sauce, steak sauce, horseradish, vinegar and brown sugar. Bring to a low boil and simmer for 5 minutes. Remove from heat and allow to cool. Place steaks in a shallow dish or pie pan, pour 1 cup sauce evenly over steaks and chill for at least 1 hour. Remove steaks from sauce and grill over glowing coals for about 6 to 8 minutes, brushing often with remaining sauce. Sprinkle with monosodium glutamate. Turn steaks and grill for another 6 minutes.

Hawaiian Short Ribs

4 lbs Lean Beef Ribs
Instant Non-seasoned Meat Tenderizer
1 lb 4 1/2 oz Can Sliced Pineapple
1/3 Cup Soy Sauce
1/3 Cup Honey
1/4 Tbsp Ginger
Hickory Wood, soaked to dampen

Cut short ribs into serving pieces. Trim excess fat from ribs. Sprinkle evenly on all sides with tenderizer. Pierce all sides deeply with long tined fork then place in single layer in baking dish. Let stand for 30 minutes at room temperature. Drain pineapple, reserving 2/3 cup syrup. In a mixing bowl, combine reserved syrup with soy sauce, honey and ginger and pour over ribs then chill for 2 to 3 hours. Remove ribs from sauce and grill, bone side down. Add dampened hickory to coals and close smoker hood. Cook slowly for 2 hours or until ribs are tender, brushing frequently with sauce. Brush pineapple rings with sauce and grill with ribs for 5 to 10 minutes. Bring remaining sauce to a boil then serve with ribs.

Beef Kabobs

1/2 Cup Lemon Juice
1/4 Cup Salad Oil
1 Onion, grated
1 tsp Salt
1/4 tsp Black Pepper
1 tsp Curry Powder
1/8 tsp Ginger
1 tsp Worcestershire Sauce
1 Bay Leaf
1 Garlic Clove, crushed
2 lb Sirloin Steak, cut into bite-sized squares
Small Mushroom Caps
Green Pepper, cut into squares
Quartered Small Tomatoes
Baby Onions

In a shallow baking dish, mix lemon juice, oil, onion, salt, pepper, curry powder, ginger, Worcestershire sauce, bay leaf and garlic in shallow pan. Add steak and mushroom caps and refrigerate for at least 4 hours, turning steak about every hour. Remove steak and mushroom caps from marinade and set remaining marinade aside to brush over kabobs while cooking. On metal skewers, alternate steak, mushrooms, green peppers, tomatoes and onions. Grill over glowing coals or broil for about 20 minutes, turning and brushing frequently with marinade.

Meatball Kabobs

2 lb Ground Beef
1/2 tsp Salt
Black Pepper to taste
1/2 tsp Garlic Salt
1 Egg, slightly beaten
1/2 lb Mushroom Caps
6 Small White Onions, Halved
16 oz Canned Potatoes
1/4 Cup Oil

Mix beef, salt, pepper, garlic salt and egg until well combined. Shape into 18 small balls. Refrigerate for at least an hour. Alternate skewering meatballs, mushrooms, onions and potatoes on metal skewer- about 3 of each will fit on a skewer. Brush with oil and grill or broil over medium coals, turn about every 3 to 4 minutes. Spread with oil at each turn. Grill until meatball is cooked through.

Fillet Mignon Kabobs

1 lb Fillet Mignon
1/2 Cup Olive Oil
3 Tbsp Red Wine Vinegar
1 tsp Thyme
1 1/2 tsp Salt
1 tsp Whole Black Pepper
Dijon Mustard

Cube fillet Mignon to large bite sized pieces and place in a glass bowl or re-sealable bag. Drizzle olive oil and red wine vinegar over meat then sprinkle with thyme, salt and pepper. Allow to marinate for 3-5 hours. Heat grill to medium high heat. Skewer meat, leaving space between each piece so it does not stick together. Lightly coat one side of meat with mustard. Broil over hot coals until center of meat reaches 140 degrees.

Ground Beef Steak and Sauce

1 1/2 lb Ground Beef
1/2 tsp Salt
1/4 tsp Pepper
2 Tbsp Worcestershire Sauce
1 tsp Garlic Salt
1 Can Cream of Mushroom Soup
1/2 Soup Can Water

Combine ground beef, salt, pepper and Worcestershire sauce. Mix well and form into patties. Broil 3 inches from heat for 5 minutes; turn and broil for about 3 minutes or until light brown. Place patties in skillet. In a small Dutch Oven or saucepan, combine garlic salt, mushroom soup and water and cook and stir until it is smooth. Pour soup mixture over beef in skillet. Heat over coals for 15 minutes until meat is cooked through. Serve on toasted rolls smothered in soup gravy or as the main dish with potatoes on the side.

Sweet Orange Chicken

6 Boneless, Skinless Chicken Breasts
1/2 Cup Honey
1 6 oz can Frozen Orange Juice Concentrate
2 Tbsp Dried Onion
1 tsp Garlic Powder
1 Tbsp Seasoning Salt
Salt
Pepper

Place chicken in a glass dish; in a separate bowl, combine remaining ingredients, mix well and pour over chicken. Cover and refrigerate overnight. Grill over medium high heat, basting often.

Sweet Ginger Citrus Pork Kabobs

1 1/2 lbs Pork-cubed
2/3 Cup Orange Juice
1/4 Cup Honey
1/2 tsp Fresh Ginger Root, grated
1/2 tsp Salt
1/4 tsp Pepper

Place pork cubes in a medium glass bowl. In a separate bowl, combine orange juice, honey, ginger, salt and pepper then mix to combine. Pour mixture over pork and refrigerate for 3 hours. Skewer meat and grill for 15 minutes, until meat is cooked through. While meat is cooking, brush with marinade. Serve with grilled pineapple.

Garlic Lime Chicken

3 Tbsp Olive Oil
3 Cloves Garlic, minced
2 Tbsp Dried Onion
3 Tbsp Lime Juice
1 Tbsp Cilantro, chopped
6 Boneless, Skinless Chicken Breasts

In a large re-sealable bag, combine olive oil, garlic, onion, lime juice and cilantro. Add chicken breast to the marinade and refrigerate for 6 hours. Grill chicken over medium heat.

Pineapple Flank Steak

4 Bacon Slices
1 Flank Steak
1 Pkg Dry Italian Salad Dressing Mix
1/4 Cup Water
1/2 Cup Pineapple Juice
1/2 Cup Vegetable Oil
1 Fresh Pineapple

Roll bacon around flank steak and secure with toothpicks placed 1 inch apart then slice in between toothpicks to make individual fillet rolls and set aside. In a
large, shallow glass dish, combine salad dressing mix,
water, pineapple juice and oil. Mix to combine
then add fillet rolls to marinate. Marinate in the refrigerator overnight (up to 24 hours). Remove dish from fridge
60 minutes before cooking to allow meat to come to
room temperature. Peel and cube pineapple. Carefully
remove toothpicks from fillet rolls and put on skewers,
alternating fillet rolls with pineapple chunks. Grill for 7
minutes per side, until meat is desired temperature.

Roy's Flank Steak on the BBQ

1/4 Cup Soy Sauce
3 Tbsp Honey
1 Tbsp White Vinegar
2 tsp Onion Powder
1 tsp Garlic Powder
1 1/2 tsp Ginger
3/4 Cup Vegetable Oil
2 Flank Steaks

In a large, shallow glass dish, combine soy sauce, honey, vinegar, onion powder, garlic powder, ginger and oil, then mix to combine. Add steaks, cover and marinate in the refrigerator for 6 hours. Grill to desired temperature.

Dill Steak

3⁄4 Cup Olive Oil
3⁄4 Cup Dill Pickle Juice
1/3 Cup sliced Dill Pickles
1 tsp minced Garlic
3 lbs London Broil Beef Steak
Salt and Pepper

In a large, shallow glass dish, combine oil, pickle juice, pickles and garlic. Add steak and coat with marinade. Cover and refrigerate overnight, for at least 8 hours, turning once. Remove meat and grill for 15 minutes. While grilling, brush with marinade to deepen flavor. Salt and pepper to taste and garnish with diced dill pickles.

Notes

Notes

Notes

Notes

Notes

Notes

Notes

Notes

Notes

Notes

Notes

Notes

Notes

Notes

Notes

Notes

Notes

Notes